LETTERS HOME from YELLOWSTONE

Lisa Halvorsen

BLACKBIRCH PRESS, INC.
WOODBRIDGE, CONNECTICUT

Published by Blackbirch Press, Inc.
260 Amity Road
Woodbridge, CT 06525

©2000 by Blackbirch Press, Inc.
First Edition

e-mail: staff@blackbirch.com
Web site: www.blackbirch.com

Printed in Singapore

10 9 8 7 6 5 4 3 2 1

All photographs ©Corel Corporation, except pages 4, 6 (left), 7 (left), 10 (left), 16 (left), 20 (left), 31 (right): ©Bert Schmitz; and pages 8 (right), 9 (left): ©National Park Service.

Library of Congress Cataloging-in-Publication Data
Halvorsen, Lisa
Yellowstone / by Lisa Halvorsen.
   p.   cm. — (Letters home from our national parks)
Includes bibliographical references and index.
Summary: This first-person account of a trip to Yellowstone National Park describes some of its outstanding features, including fiery geysers, boiling mud pools, and diverse wildlife.
ISBN 1-56711-465-2
1. Yellowstone National Park—Juvenile literature. [1. Yellowstone National Park. 2. National parks and reserves.] I. Title.
F722 .H26 2000
917.87'520433—dc21   00-008277

TABLE OF CONTENTS

Arrival in Mammoth Hot Springs 4
Mammoth Hot Springs 6
Lamar Valley 6
Baronette Peak 8
Yellowstone River Canyon 12
Yellowstone Falls 13
Norris Geyser Basin 14
Firehole River 16
Midway Geyser Basin 17
Castle Geyser 18
Biscuit Basin 19
Pine Trees and Wildflowers 20
Fairyslippers and Paintbrushes 21
Old Faithful 22
Wildlife 24
Yellowstone Lake/Snake River ...30-31
Glossary 32
For More Information 32
Index 32

Arrival in . . .

Mammoth Hot Springs

Many visitors start their trip at park headquarters in Mammoth Hot Springs like we did. There, we saw an exhibit on Yellowstone's history. I learned that General Henry Washburn's expedition came to the area in 1870. They were amazed by what they saw. A year later the director of the U.S. Geological Survey, Dr. Ferdinand Hayden, explored the region. He brought artist Thomas Moran and photographer William Henry Jackson with him. Together, they convinced Congress to establish Yellowstone National Park in 1872.

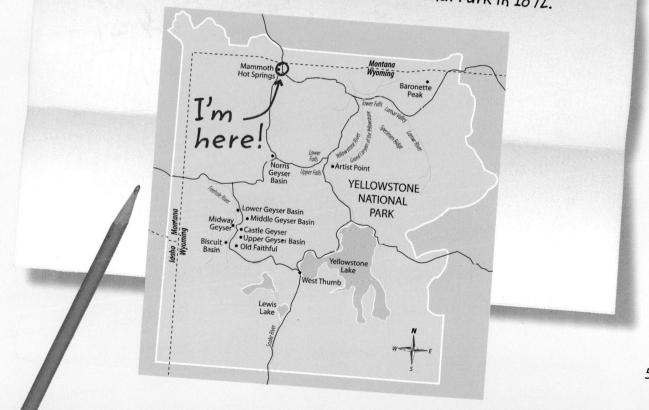

Mammoth Hot Springs

A ranger at the visitor's center told us that Jim Bridger, a famous mountain man, once called Mammoth Hot Springs a "petrified rainbow." I was amazed at the gorgeous colors in the hot springs. The limestone terraces are shades of pink, yellow, orange, green, and brown. The colors were created by micro-organisms and bacteria.

Mammoth Hot Springs

Limestone terraces

Travertine deposits

Mammoth Hot Springs

I think Mammoth Hot Springs looks like the mountain is turning itself inside out. In a way, it actually is. The hot springs bring up water from limestone beds hundreds of feet below. The springs deposit the lime-filled water as travertine, a light-colored, banded mineral. The terraces build up at a rate of 6 to 12 inches a year!

Lamar Valley

We decided to travel east from Mammoth Hot Springs to Lamar Valley. My guidebook says that the area was named for Lucius Lamar, the Secretary of the Interior during President Cleveland's first administration.

On the edge of Lamar Valley, we passed a place called Specimen Ridge. It contains the largest fossil forest in the world. There are more than 100 different species of plants and trees. In fact, the area has more petrified (stone) trees—including huge redwoods—than any other area in the world!

Sunset, Lamar Valley

Specimen Ridge

Specimen Ridge

Rolling hills, Lamar Valley

The petrified forest is buried in 27 layers of volcanic ash from eruptions that happened 45 to 50 million years ago!

The entire Lamar Valley has great geological interest. Some of the oldest rock outcrops in Yellowstone are found in the Lamar River Canyon. Geologists believe the gneiss and schist (metamorphic rocks) were formed more than 2 billion years ago!

I read that in 1870, a group of prospectors went searching for gold in the Lamar Valley. Although they reported several encounters with grizzly bears, they never found gold.

Lamar Valley

I also read that a Native American tribe related to the Shoshone—the Sheepeaters—once lived in this area of the park. They hunted bighorn sheep for food and used their horns to make bows. To reach their hunting grounds, they followed the Bannock Trail, in the northern part of Yellowstone. This trail was used by many tribes for more than 11,000 years to hunt bison and other animals!

Bison herd

Winter in Lamar Valley

Lamar Valley

Young elk

Today, Lamar Valley is one of the best places in the park to watch wildlife. I was glad to learn that, in 1880, the valley was set aside as a game reserve to protect deer, elk, antelope, and bighorn sheep. From the road, we spotted a herd of elk munching on grasses. They didn't seem to mind that I was watching them through my binoculars. Many bears and wolves also live here.

Baronette Peak

As we continued along the northern route, we stopped briefly to photograph majestic Baronette Peak. According to my guidebook, the 10,404-foot-tall peak was named in 1878 for C. J. "Yellowstone Jack" Baronett. He was a famous early explorer. On official maps at the time, the name was mistakenly spelled Baronette.

Baronette Peak is one of more than 20 mountains in Yellowstone with an elevation above 10,000 feet. I wasn't surprised to see snow covering its peak. The average elevation in Yellowstone is about 7,000 feet, so many of the park's highest peaks, including Baronette, are covered with snow much of the year.

Baronette Peak

Yellowstone River Canyon

Did you know that Yellowstone has a "grand canyon?" We saw it today when we drove along Grand Loop Road. The canyon has steep, colorful walls of rhyolite (a type of granite formed from lava). The walls slope down to a churning river. It roars down a V-shaped canyon that's 20 miles long, about 1,200 feet deep, and up to 4,000 feet wide.

My guidebook says that the canyon was formed by the Yellowstone River more than 10,000 years ago! The Minnetaree Indians used the word "Mitse-a-da-zi" to describe the bluffs. Early French Canadian trappers translated this name into "Rive des Roches Jaunes," or "river of yellow rock." That soon became "Yellow stone."

Yellowstone River Canyon

Yellowstone Falls

I think the most interesting features in the canyon are the waterfalls. The highest waterfall in the park is found here. Lower Falls has a 308-foot drop. That's nearly twice the height of Niagara Falls! Upper Falls, at 109 feet, is not as high, but it is just as impressive.

We stopped at the overlooks along the canyon rim to snap photos. The best view was from Artist Point. That's where Thomas Moran painted his famous picture of this canyon and waterfall. It is now on display at the Department of Interior Museum in Washington, D.C.

Yellowstone Falls

View near
Artist Point

Thomas Moran also painted Tower Fall at the northern end of the Grand Canyon of Yellowstone. There are some strange-looking volcanic pinnacles (high peaks) around the top of this 132-foot-high waterfall.

About halfway between the Upper and Lower falls, Crystal Falls tumbles over the north rim. The best view of this fall is from the North Rim Trail.

Norris Geyser Basin

Next we headed to the thermal basins. According to the guide, the park has more than 10,000 thermal features. There are geysers, fumaroles (volcanic holes), hot springs, and mud pots. They all have one thing in common. They smell like rotten eggs! That's from the sulfur.

The term geyser, which means "to gush," comes from Iceland. That's where geysers were first discovered. About 60% of all geysers in the world are found in Yellowstone.

Norris Geyser Basin is the most active geyser basin in Yellowstone. The basin is home to Steamboat Geyser, the world's tallest active geyser. It also has Echinus, the world's largest acid geyser. Its water is as acidic as lemon juice!

Norris Geyser Basin

Visitors at Norris Geyser

Firehole River

Yellowstone is located on what's called a hot spot. That's a place where Earth's shifting plates meet and push magma up to the surface. Our guide also explained that much of Yellowstone, including the thermal basins, sits inside remains of an ancient volcano. The collapsed crater is called a caldera, which means "cauldron" in Spanish.

The Firehole River flows through this area, linking the Upper and Lower geyser basins. Early trappers thought the steam rising from the river was smoke from a fire. The steam comes from hot springs in the riverbed. We saw bison and elk feeding along this river.

Firehole River

Midway Geyser Basin

At Midway Geyser Basin, we joined a ranger-led walk to learn about the thermal activity in this area. We followed the boardwalk to a huge, boiling crater that used to be a geyser, once called the Excelsior Geyser. It last erupted in 1888. We also saw Grand Prismatic Spring. At 370 feet in diameter, it is the largest hot spring in the entire park. It is also one of the most colorful. We learned that the color comes from algae. You can tell how hot the water is by the color of the algae living in it! A pale yellow or pink color means scalding hot—180 degrees Fahrenheit or hotter.

I was also amazed to learn that scientists use the microscopic life forms in Yellowstone's hot springs to do medical research. They use it for DNA "fingerprinting" in criminal investigations.

Midway Geyser Basin

Castle Geyser

Like Old Faithful, Castle Geyser is one of only a handful of geysers in the park that erupts "on schedule." It erupts through a 12-foot-high cone that looks like the ruins of a medieval castle. It usually goes off every 9 to 11 hours. For the first 20 minutes, it shoots water into the air. That's followed by 40 minutes of steam.

Castle Geyser

Castle Geyser

Biscuit Basin

On our walking tour, we also saw Biscuit Basin, part of the Upper Geyser Basin. It was named for the odd biscuit-shaped formations that were once found near Sapphire Pool. These formations disappeared in August 1959 when a major earthquake rocked the park. The earthquake was not centered in the park, but it still caused several rock slides.

The ranger told us that earthquakes can cause changes in the eruption cycles of geysers. Jewel Geyser is the main geyser in Biscuit Basin. After the 1959 earthquake, it spouted continuously. Now it erupts about every 10 minutes, sending up 7 to 8 bursts.

Biscuit Basin

Boardwalk at Biscuit Basin

Pine Trees and Wildflowers

More than two-thirds of the park is forested. The most common tree is the lodgepole pine. It can grow up to 75 feet tall. It is also called the jack pine. About 80% of the forests in Yellowstone are made up of this species.

Many of the other trees in Yellowstone are evergreens. You can find sub-alpine fir, Englemann spruce, and juniper. They are found mostly at higher elevations. At lower elevations aspen, cottonwood, red birch, and alder are more common.

Many hills are covered with penstemon flowers, which bloom in the summer.

Aspens

Penstemon flowers

Fairyslippers and Paintbrushes

In 1988, there was a terrible fire in the park. More than 25,000 firefighters were called in to put out the blaze. By the time they did, about nearly half the park—1.4 million acres—had been destroyed by fire. The next year wildflowers, including blue lupines, Canterbury bells, and Indian paintbrush grew up through the ashes. I especially liked the Indian paintbrush. Legend says that a Native American was trying to paint a prairie sunset. He gave up in frustration and threw down his brush. Where it landed, this colorful flower grew.

Lupine hillside

Indian paintbrush

Mountain grasses

Yellowstone's trees

The official park flower is the gentian. It's a fringed, purple flower. It blooms from June to September. More than a dozen orchids also grow in Yellowstone, including the fairyslipper orchid. It looks like a lady's shoe! It is found in the shady, forested areas.

In midsummer, the mountain meadows are covered with clover, phlox, forget-me-nots, alpine buttercups, and other miniature, flowering plants.

Old Faithful

Earlier today, while waiting for Old Faithful to erupt, we listened to the ranger describe this geyser. We learned that it is a cone-type geyser that erupts every 35 to 120 minutes. It can spout as high as 180 feet. The eruption can last from as little as 30 seconds to as long as 5 minutes. You know when it's about to erupt because you can actually hear Old Faithful rumble.

The ranger said that the water that spouts from Old Faithful fell as rainwater 500 years ago! Records of Old Faithful's eruptions have been kept every year since 1870.

Old Faithful

Old Faithful eruption

Geyser eruption

Old Faithful is my favorite, but many people think nearby Grand Geyser is more spectacular. Grand Geyser usually erupts every 8 to 12 hours, reaching 150 to 180 feet high. The eruptions last about 12 minutes.

After Old Faithful put on its show, we followed the boardwalk to see other attractions in the Upper Geyser Basin. This 1-square-mile basin has more than 100 geysers and many hot springs! I really liked the paint pots. These steaming mud pools actually look like boiling pots of paint. The view of the basin from Geyser Hill on the other side of Firehole River made me think of how the early explorers must have felt.

Wildlife

I can't decide which I like better—the geysers or the animals. The wildlife is incredible. In fact, Yellowstone is called the largest game preserve in the country. I believe it!

As we drove through the thermal areas, we had to stop twice to let small herds of bison cross the road in front of us. These mighty animals each weigh more than half a ton and stand 6 feet tall at the shoulder. In the early days of the West, they were slaughtered by the thousands, mostly for their woolly hides. By 1900, fewer than 50 were left. Today the Yellowstone herd numbers in the thousands, thanks to conservation efforts.

Bison

Grizzly bear family

Pronghorn antelope

Coyote

The gray wolf was completely eliminated from the park by the early 1920s. It was killed to protect other wildlife and livestock. After it was re-introduced in 1995, the park once again had all the animal species it originally had when John Colter, the first American to see the thermal areas, arrived in 1807.

Can you guess which park mammal is the fastest? The park naturalist told us it is the pronghorn antelope. It can run up to 60 miles an hour.

Wildlife

There are between 300 and 600 grizzly bears in Yellowstone. Adult males average 350 pounds, but some can weigh as much as 800 pounds. Females range in weight from 200 to 400 pounds.

In the 1960s, two brothers, Frank and John Craighead, were the first to put radio collars on the bears. They did this to track the bears' migration, hibernation, and mating habits.

Coyotes, bobcats, mule deer, yellow-bellied marmots, elk, and black bears are also among the 60 types of mammals found in the park.

Grizzly bear

Mule deer

Bull elk

Bald eagle

More than 300 species of birds have also been reported in Yellowstone. People have sighted everthing from tiny songbirds to the 4-foot-tall sandhill crane.

You can usually spot bald eagles, white pelicans, and trumpeter swans along the rivers and near Yellowstone Lake.

If you are lucky, you might even see a whooping crane. This is one of the most endangered species in North America.

Yellowstone Lake

Today we took a scenic boat cruise on Yellowstone Lake. It's the largest mountain lake in North America. It is located 7,733 feet above sea level!

The captain told us that Yellowstone Lake is 20 miles long by 14 miles wide. It has 110 miles of shoreline. The average depth is 140 feet. The deepest point in the lake is an underwater canyon near Stevenson Island. It is 390 feet deep. The canyon was found by a small submersible robot-powered submarine. In the early 1990s, underwater geysers were first discovered near West Thumb.

Yellowstone Lake

Snake River

Several rivers flow through Yellowstone. One of them, the Snake River, is the fourth-largest river in the country. Its headwaters are near the Continental Divide on Two Ocean Plateau. That's a perfect name, since water divides there and heads either toward the Pacific or Atlantic Ocean.

The Snake River is a favorite fishing place—not only for people but also for osprey and eagles! It was named for the "Snake" or Shoshone Indians.

Now that I've seen Yellowstone, I understand why no one believed the tales of the early explorers. From its fiery geysers to its boiling mud pools and unusual wildlife, Yellowstone truly is one of the most incredible places on Earth!

Snake River

Snake River

Glossary

Continental Divide ridge of the Rocky Mountains that separates rivers that flow in an easterly direction from those that flow in a westerly direction.

Fumarole a vent in a volcanic region from which gases and vapors arise.

Geyser a hot spring or fountain that shoots water and steam into the air from time to time.

Headwaters the source and upper part of a river or stream.

Mammal a warm-blooded animal that is able to produce milk to feed its young.

Travertine a light-colored mineral formed by deposits of lime from spring waters or hot springs.

For More Information

Benson, Marjorie. *Yellowstone* (Wonders of the World). Chatham, NJ: Raintree/Steck Vaughn, 1995.

Gallant, Roy. *Geysers: When Earth Roars* (First Book). Danbury, CT: Franklin Watts, Inc., 1997.

Holmes, Burton. Fred Israel. *Yellowstone* (World 100 Years Ago). New York, NY: Chelsea House Publishing, 2000.

Marron, Carol. *Yellowstone*. Glendale, CA: Crestwood House, 1989.

Web Site
Yellowstone National Park

This official web site of the park features a kids' activity section, as well as provides information on wildlife, history, and trip planning—www.nps.gov/yell/home.htm

Index

Algae, 18

Antelope, 11, 27

Artist Point, 14

Bannock Trail, 10

Baronett, C.J. "Yellowstone Jack," 12

Baronette Peak, 12

Bears, 9, 11, 26, 28

Bighorn sheep, 10, 11

Birds, 29

Biscuit Basin, 20

Bison, 10, 17, 26

Bobcats, 28

Bridger, Jim, 6

Canyon, 9, 13, 14, 15, 30

Colter, John, 25

Congress, 5

Coyotes, 28

Craighead, Frank, 28

Craighead, John, 28

Deer, 11, 28

Department of Interior, 14

Eagles, 29, 31

Earthquakes, 20

Elk, 11, 17, 29

Fire, 22

Firehole River, 17, 25

Fossil, 8

General Henry Washburn, 5

Gentian, 23

Geyser Hill, 25

Geysers, 16, 20, 25, 26, 30, 31

Castle, 19

Echinus, 16

Excelsior, 18

Grand, 25

Jewel, 20

Old Faithful, 19, 24, 25

Steamboat, 16

Grand Prismatic Spring, 18

Hayden, Ferdinand, 5

Hot spot, 17

Indian paintbrush, 22

Jackson, William Henry, 5

Lamar, Lucius, 8

Lamar River Canyon, 9

Lamar Valley, 8, 9, 10, 11

Limestone, 6, 7

Mammoth Hot Springs, 5, 6, 7, 8

Marmots, 28

Micro-organisms, 6

Midway Geyser Basin, 18

Minnetaree Indians, 13

Moran, Thomas, 5, 14, 15

Norris Geyser Basin, 16

North Rim Trail, 15

Orchids, 23

Paint pots, 25

Penstemon flowers, 21

Petrified, 6, 8, 9

Rhyolite, 13

Sapphire Pool, 20

Shoshone Indians, 10, 31

Snake River, 31

Specimen Ridge, 8, 9

Stevenson Island, 30

Trees, 8, 21, 23

Washington, D.C., 14

Waterfalls, 14

Crystal Falls, 15

Lower Falls, 14, 15

Tower Falls, 15

Upper Falls, 14, 15

Upper Geyser Basin, 17, 20, 25

Wildflowers, 21, 22

Wolves, 11, 27

Yellowstone Lake, 29, 30

Yellowstone River, 13

79133